Daughter of Bangladesh
Witnesses Tahrir Emancipation

In Egypt: A Country that was Rocked by a Revolution

Sharmin Ahmad

Copyright © 2012 by Sharmin Ahmad. 115905-AHMA
Illustration Concept: Sharmin Ahmad

Library of Congress Control Number: 2012908814

ISBN: Softcover   978-1-4771-1324-0
       Hardcover   978-1-4771-1325-7

All rights reserved. No part of this book may be reproduced or transmitted in any form or by any means, electronic or mechanical, including photocopying, recording, or by any information storage and retrieval system, without permission in writing from the copyright owner.

To order additional copies of this book, contact:
Xlibris Corporation
1-888-795-4274
www.Xlibris.com
Orders@Xlibris.com

Dedication

To my beloved husband Amr for all your love and inspiration.
You have brought Egypt close to my heart.

Acknowledgements

My deepest thanks to the octogenarian Albert Mondle for graciously typing the story in an amazing speed which I originally wrote and published it in Bangla; Maswood Alam Khan for his enthusiasm and commitment in translating this story from Bangla into English, Kareema Abdul-Basir, Dr. Sharon Mijares And Dr. Amr Khairy Abdalla for their excellent editorial support. I would also like to thank the X-libris publisher for offering all the support I have received in transforming the story into a published book.

To Dearest Uncle Mondle,
My heartfelt thanks for all your inspiration & gracious help but are great gift to a writer's spirit.
Love, light & peace
Sharmin Ahmad
December 6, 2012

Daughter of Bangladesh Liberation Witnesses

Tahrir Emancipation

In Egypt: a country that was rocked by a revolution

Sharmin Ahmad

A New Beginning

It was a pleasant spring evening in 1998 when I first met my life's companion – my husband, Amr Khairy Abdalla. Amr had taken a seat next to me and my mother (Mrs. Zohra Tajuddin) at a human rights award ceremony in the state of Virginia, U.S.A. As she conversed with Amr, my mother became quite impressed with him. The thought occurred to her that this gentleman might be a perfect life partner for me. This proved to be an example of a "mother's intuition." Later on, when Amr proposed marriage, our married life began with my mother's blessings.

My parents: Father Tajuddin Ahmad and mother Syeda Zohra Tajuddin. Dhaka, Bangladesh, 1974.

Amr and I on our wedding day: Casablanca Restaurant, Old Town Alexandria, Virginia, USA, October 7, 1998.

Amr was born and raised in Egypt. After completing a law degree, he began his career in Cairo as a public prosecutor. Later, pursuing a new direction in the United States, he earned a Doctor of Philosophy degree from George Mason University in Virginia in the field of "Conflict Resolution and Peace Studies". He worked for many years teaching these subjects at George Mason University and other institutions.

There are many people diligently working for greater peace in this world, and Amr is one of them. He is now Vice Rector of the University for Peace (UPEACE) in Costa Rica where he continues to lecture on peace and conflict resolution. UPEACE is an international institution mandated by the United Nations in 1980. It is a unique seat of learning that was established with the goal of promoting a global spirit of understanding, tolerance and peaceful coexistence. Amr's position has led him to visit many corners of the world. During the last four years he has traveled to the five continents, including my motherland Bangladesh. The main objective of his travels is to encourage fraternity among the students and teachers of the universities in the countries he visits in order to establish a model of learning that can foster peaceful conflict resolution around the world. He is a diligent worker and is deeply committed to this objective. His work has already earned him honor and recognition.

Whenever the topic of Egypt was broached in his presence, Amr would react with intense concern. I used to hear him say, "as long as the dictatorial government in Egypt continuously robbed its people of their rights, a road to peace and development in my homeland would never be established." These thoughts were never far from his mind. He believed that "once a solid foundation of education and public awareness of their rights could be established in Egypt, the construction of the framework for a democratic system would be an inevitable corollary." His desire for a better Egypt drove him to visit his homeland time and time again. While in Egypt he would lay out a variety of academic plans and training programs, in an effort to assist with Egypt's transformation. The pending reality of a fair and just Egypt had become a guiding motivator in his life.

I was in Bangladesh on the 25th of January when I got the news of the unprecedented mass revolution in Egypt. Amr was in Egypt at that time, but I was unable to communicate with him until the 29th of January. Hosni Mubarak's government had severed all the communication channels of mobile phones, land phones and Internet. It took four days, until Saturday the 29th, before Amr somehow managed to communicate with me from a land phone in a hotel in Cairo. I could hear the hope and inspiration in his voice, but also a sense of apprehension and despair. The police had fired shots at peaceful demonstrations in Suez and other areas. Scores of unarmed people were being killed. To protest against the killings of the civilians, thousands of people took to the streets in Tahrir Square on Friday, the 28th of January, a day the revolutionaries had designated as the "Friday of Fury". On the previous day, in Alexandria, Amr had held a meeting with his students about preventing religious violence in the aftermath of the church bombing in Alexandria on New Year's Eve. Many of his students had participated in the protests on the streets of Cairo the days before. All of them were determined to make a success of the revolution even at the sacrifice of their lives.

The Foundation for a Revolution

The determination of Egypt's youth was the result of preparations that had been underway in different phases for more that three years. In 2008, a student group named "The April 6th" was formed to voice support for textile workers experiencing discrimination. This first stepping-stone of the mass revolution was in fact laid in Alexandria, a historic city that was established by the world conqueror, Alexander the Great, and was the adored home of Egypt's legendary Queen Cleopatra.

In June of 2010, a young man named Khaled Saeed, also an inhabitant of Alexandria, died from brutal torture while he was in police custody. In a fiery protest against the murder of Khaled, another Egyptian youth, Wael Ghonim, who was Head of Marketing at Google in the Middle East & North Africa, launched his famous Facebook page. Writing that "We are all Khaled Saeed", he helped spark the revolution through internet-based social networking. The number of members who initially subscribed to his Facebook page rose to 50,000 in a matter of 24 hours and by January 2011 the number had skyrocketed to 300,000 with members coming mainly from Suez, Aswan and Cairo.

In spite of having no affiliation with any political party, youths like Wael Ghonim who are by nature vociferous against injustices, showed that they could launch successful mass revolutions - like that, which followed in Tunisia - driven only by their conscience. The online social network Facebook had turned out to be an essential tool for the making of a successful peaceful revolution----an extraordinary event that has been the first of its kind in the history of the world.

The Egyptian Police Day, the 25th of January, was chosen as the Day of Protest against police brutality. Here again, it was on Facebook that workshops were organized. Training was provided on how to observe the Day of Protest by carrying out actions that circumvented the paths of direct clashes with the security forces. Facebook was uploaded with detailed information about arrangements for treatment of the injured, along with lists of lawyers and physicians who might be needed in case of police harassment or torture - with their contact numbers and specialties duly mentioned.

The creative application of social media for the purpose of supporting a peaceful mass revolution was marvelously demonstrated as a huge crowd of 30,000 people gathered in Tahrir (Liberation) Square in Cairo. On the same day, a total of about one million protesters congregated in a multitude of mass demonstrations held in different parts of Egypt. People of varied opinions coming from all social strata joined in with their fellow brothers and sisters to voice their loudest ever protests against injustice, crime and dictatorship. The whole world watched in awe as the daily episodes of the revolution gathered momentum for eighteen days. Beamed live through satellites to audiences all over the globe, a new chapter in the history of mass revolutions was introduced to the world.

Amr braved an adventure on the night of January 29 as he departed from Egypt to his previously planned workshop in Ethiopia amidst the chaos and confusion that had almost brought the Cairo airport to a standstill. I had just returned to the United States and was very busy working a tight schedule in my first two weeks at home. All the same, I tried to keep abreast of the latest situation in Egypt. I would tune in to CNN and Al Jazeera television channels and correspond through email with my friends in Egypt whenever I had a chance. This way I could keep a close watch on what was happening in Cairo. From Alexandria, Yasmine Fakhry wrote: "I thought the nation of Egypt was deep asleep. Oh no! I was wrong. The Cairo revolution has proven my idea to be completely erroneous."

Hosni Mubarak, the long time dictator of Egypt, ultimately abdicated. He resigned on Friday, the 11th of February. Amr, meanwhile, had left Ethiopia and already returned to his work in Costa Rica. I was busy packing as I was planning to go to Costa Rica on the 18th of February. But, on the 14th of February, Amr telephoned me to express his wishes for me on Valentine's Day! I was thrilled to hear his voice. And then Amr said: "As my gift to you on Valentine's Day I want to escort you all the way to the newly liberated Egypt." I shouted back: "When, will we go?" He replied: "On the 16th." He continued: "On Friday, the 18th of February, we both will join in with an ocean of people at Tahrir Square where the celebration of 'Juma't al Nasr', meaning 'Friday of Victory', will take place. We will walk together, hand-in-hand, through Egypt's 'Liberation Square'."

In the past, Amr had given me many a gift of pleasant surprises on special occasions. But, the gift on this Valentine's Day was unique indeed. Amr's gift combined personal affection with collective joy. As I was anticipating our joint trip to the newly liberated Egypt, I experienced a vivid memory of my Father's sayings in which he expressed his firm belief that: "The slavery of a nation casts a dark shadow of subjugation for the whole of humanity and the liberty of a nation unleashes a dazzling floodlight of freedom for the whole of mankind."

February 17, 2011

We reached Cairo Thursday night, on the 17th of February. Leaving our luggage in the hotel room, Amr took me to his favorite childhood restaurant to treat me to Feteer, a special Egyptian food. It was only half an hour walk from our hotel.

The weather was excellent with temperatures hovering around sixty degrees Fahrenheit! Weather in Egypt remains quite pleasant from October through April - the best time to visit. Wearing a jacket or simply a sweater, one can comfortably stroll around under the open sky in Cairo on a February evening. As we walked in the desert breeze, my body recovered from the numbness of the long plane flight. The restaurant, which was now run by the son of the owner, was simple and basic, but it pulsed with lively warmth that you usually don't feel in a chic eatery. It had gained popularity especially for Feteer in Heliopolis, the neighborhood where Amr had grown up.

Feteer is prepared in almost the same way as Mughlai Paratha, a Bangladeshi-Indian Subcontinent delicacy. The dough for both recipes is made with flour, oil, salt, milk, etc., and pressed out on a rolling board with a rolling pin. In the case of Feteer, the dough has to be pressed very thin, to a size almost half the thickness of Mughlai Paratha. A little water is added to soften the dough, and flour is periodically sprinkled on the dough while thinning it to prevent it from sticking to the board. Once the thinned dough is ready, a filling of beaten eggs, coriander leaves, minced meat, sausage, olive, cheese, etc. (in accordance with an individual customer's selection) is placed on the thin sheet of the dough and folded inside. The stuffed dough is now baked at 300 to 400 degrees Fahrenheit for about two-three minutes in the live fire of a Tandoor oven, a cylindrical clay oven with heat generated by charcoal. Sweet Feteer is not made from stuffed dough; but instead the rolled plain dough is first baked in the oven and then topped with cream of milk and sugar.

The art of making feteer!

Another very popular Egyptian delicacy is Kushari, which is similar to the Khichuri of Bangladesh. Later, I came to learn that Khichuri of our subcontinent traveled all the way to the Arab world and became known in Egypt by the local name Kushari. Both words, Kushari and Khichuri, are almost identically pronounced and their ingredients of rice, lentils, fried onions, garlic, etc., are similar. While Bangladeshis know the tamarind as Tetul, the Arabs call it Tamr-hind. The Arabic word Tamr-hind means "the date of Hind (or India)" and the English word Tamarind has evolved etymologically from the Arabic Tamr-hind. In spite of diverse differences in the appearances and cultures of the people of this planet, these commonalities of language and food point out to the strings of relationship that integrate the whole of humankind.

After filling our bellies with Feteer, we set out at 1:00 am to walk back to La Meridian Hotel in Heliopolis. On the way we purchased a number of newspapers and drank fresh sugarcane juice bought from a roadside shop. Many shops had kept their doors open and pedestrians were still out on the town. After we had returned to our hotel we learned, to our surprise, that a curfew had been in force since twelve o'clock, midnight. We laughed as we recognized that this one-of-a kind curfew was a part of Egypt's victory celebration.

February 18, 2011

The next day was Friday, a sunlit day that was glowing with anticipation. The temperature was in the neighborhood of seventy degrees Fahrenheit. Amr's eldest brother Alaa Khairy Abdalla, a retired armed forces officer, came with his car to drive us to the Tahrir Square. With his lively looks radiating his immense delight at the coming of this day, it was difficult to believe that Alaa was ill, suffering from kidney failure that had kept him dependent on dialysis for over a year. His joy at what was taking place in his beloved country was stronger than his ailment. Mustafa, Alaa's 19-year old son, had already gone to Tahrir Square where he, along with his friends, were participating in the work of cleansing the adjoining roads of trash that had accumulated during the demonstrations. Liberated Egypt that had been completely freed of dictatorial rule at the cost of blood and sacrifice of hundreds was now in the hands of its people. It had become the responsibility of each and every citizen to rebuild Egypt, to keep it neat and clean, and to guard his or her country's future.

Tahrir Square is in the vicinity of Cairo National Museum in the downtown area. Alaa parked his car in the shade of a tree about a mile from the square. Unlike in many other countries where an acute lack of security makes it difficult to leave a car parked without a driver in attendance, most of Cairo's residents leave their cars parked on the street unattended. Car hijacking is quite commonplace in many other countries, but overall Egypt is much safer.

With the car safely parked, we started walking towards the Tahrir Square in down town Cairo. It was already 11:00 in the late morning. There were checkpoints with armed forces deployed on all of the roads leading to the downtown sections. At one such checkpoint Amr and Alaa showed their identity cards. One officer wanted to see my ID also, but Amr said: "She is my wife." The young officer with respect and a pleasant smile said in a soft tone: "If she is your wife then I am her brother!" The officer opened the pathway for us saying "Ahlan wa Sahlan," meaning "you're family and you are welcome," a traditional welcoming greeting used in the Arab world when one opens up a door for his guests.

With a group of youth cleaning around Tahrir Square.

We could see young men and women organizing into groups throughout Tahrir Square in order to sweep roads and pavements. Some were holding brooms and others were carrying buckets. Some people on the roadside were selling Egyptian flags, lapel pins and small tags with slogans. Feeling in harmony with this effort, we also bought a few flags and tags. On one such tag, with a short rope meant for hanging around one's neck, the words: "Huriya, Adal, Musawa," meaning "Freedom, Justice, Equality," were engraved in Arabic.

A citizen holding a banner which reads: "No to military courts for civilian politicians."

Human right activists were holding up big posters as reminder of the gruesome human rights violations that took place under the Mubaraq regime. All of the shops in and around the square were open. Other stores selling expensive furniture, electronics, apparels and perfumes were also gradually re-opening. However, some of our acquaintances didn't turn out to participate in the victory celebration at Tahrir Square on hearing rumors about possible clashes with the Mubarak loyalists. Our conversations with shopkeepers assured us that they were not apprehensive about any disturbances. One merchant proudly informed us that he, and many other shopkeepers like him, had participated in the 18-day long peaceful demonstrations by setting up blockades to seize control of the country. During the blockade, demonstrators who camped in Tahrir Square were supplied with free necessities like foods and drinks from those same shops.

As Tahrir Square began to resonate with the celebrations of the jubilant crowd, a group of camel drivers suddenly entered the square. Their appearance came as a complete surprise, but this time the intention of the camel drivers was very different from their earlier invasion of the square on the 2nd of February. On that day, which is still remembered as a day of horror, camels and horses were used to attack peaceful anti-Mubarak demonstrators. However, at this moment the camel drivers had come to seek forgiveness. Sincerely soliciting absolution from the Egyptian people, they distributed thousands of flyers among the celebrators. They said that the functionaries of the then Mubarak government had compelled them to attack the demonstrators. The drivers chose the next day, Saturday, the 19th of February, as the day for soliciting forgiveness. The camel drivers invited the people to join with them in observing that day. It should be mentioned here that some camel drivers, who were not the least bit concerned about politics and liberty, had feared, during the mass revolution in early February, that they might lose their means of earning sufficient income to buy food for themselves and their animals if Cairo's continuous demonstrations discouraged the return of tourists to Egypt.

Someone in the crowd made a poignant comment: "This mass revolution has also helped us to express the beautiful facets of our character." While observing the revelry in Tahrir Square from the comfort of a roadside shaded tree or standing on the pavement we felt we were witnessing the rebirth of an emancipated nation regaining its pride, will and self-confidence.

A makeshift memorial in the middle of Tahrir Square for martyrs of the revolution.

The banner demands "retribution" against the ousted president Mubarak and his minister of interior Habib al Adli.

Celebrating Victory!

    The dedication to true democracy was immense. In the melee of people walking about in all directions were men and women who had painted their faces with the Egyptian flag. Some youths, who were most probably Christians, were singing while wandering around with the name of Jesus Christ (peace be upon him) painted in English on their cheeks. Those who had embraced martyrdom during the revolution included Christians, Muslims, men, women and even children. Above all, irrespective of their age, religion, color, creed and sex, they were all Egyptians. It was a revolution of the Egyptian nation.

17

With my husband Amr (in red shirt in the middle) and his brother Alaa.

The banner reads: "Hero Martyrs: rest [in peace]! Your blood has not gone to waste.

People creatively making use of any space for the Friday mid-day prayer in Tahrir Square.

Pictures of some of the martyrs of the revolution.

Celebration!

Just in front of us we saw a procession of women with Egyptian flags in their hands and huge white banners above their heads. Some of the banners had the slogan: "Egypt: Land of Pharaoh; Land of Freedom" printed in English upon them. Another banner was inscribed with the phrase: "Egypt! Land of the 1st Revolution of the 21st Century."

Although it was in Tunisia that the first revolution in the Arab world took place, Egypt, a nation of eighty million people constituted the largest populous country in the Middle East and North Africa. It is considered to be a great nation given her seven thousand year old heritage, rich history and strategic position. That is why the revolution in Egypt attracted so much worldwide attention.

Lost in the ocean of millions of people, as we were observing their celebrations we became part of their history. We were in fact participating in history in the making. From a shop adjacent to the footpath where we were standing, a shopkeeper invited us inside. He said: "If your legs ache from standing you may please take a little rest sitting on chairs inside my shop".

Azan for Jumma prayer (call for Friday prayer) was heralded a few minutes after 12 at midday. The Jumma prayer would be led by Yusuf al-Qaradawi, the Imam (worship leader in a mosque) who is a famous Islamic thinker, a renowned scholar and a prolific writer. Author of hundreds of books on Islam and best known for his program ash-Shariah wal-Hayat ("Shariah and Life"), broadcast on Al Jazeera, Imam Yusuf has earned fame and respect at home and abroad for his way of presenting Islam in the light of modern age, his powerful writings and his support for democracy and free elections in the Middle East. But his activism and freethinking had also earned him the wrath of Egypt's dictator, resulting in many years of exile He has now returned to his liberated homeland.

The Jumma prayer started with all the congregated Muslims standing in disciplined rows. As prayer rugs were not readily available many people laid their Egyptian flags and banners on the road, setting a place for prayer. The lady next to me extended her flag for me to share in my praying. In front of Allah, the Provident, men and women standing on the same ground had no difference. Normally, men and women are separated for prayers. Today, gender differences were irrelevant as all joined together in the same space and with the same mission. The prayer ended with gratitude paid to God.

Tears rolled down the cheeks of a lady who also stood next to me. Her name is Fatima. I wanted to know why she was crying. She replied in clear English: "On this historic day of victory I am terribly missing my children." I asked her where her children lived. Fatima told me her children lived in the United States; one, her son, lives in Maryland and the other, her daughter, in Virginia. I told her that I live in Maryland too.

We exchanged our phone numbers while we were still standing amidst the crowd. I told her I would communicate with her children when I would go back to the United States. After the Jumma prayer the Tahrir Square once again became resonant with three million people chanting slogans that continued to reverberate through the air above the square ground. Amr and Alaa in unison with the fellow Egyptians chanted slogans in rhyme: "Erfa Rasak Fo', Enta Masry" (Stand with your head held high, you are Egyptian). My mind in no time traveled back to the day on the 16th of December in 1971—the day when our joys also knew no bound in our own homeland Bangladesh which had been just liberated from the occupying Pakistan military regime. This was the day when the Bangladeshi people once again could stand with their heads held high!

Slowly we walked away from the Tahrir Square, still chanting slogans. On huge billboards all around the streets were hung the photographs of the recent martyrs. Bent over on the roadside, a man was writing inspirational poems and slogans on a poster. Youths, accompanied by their bands, were singing patriotic songs. Many people, in remembrance of the more than 400 victims of the revolution, were offering poems that they had composed themselves.

People expressing via drawings and poetry their demands for justice and determination to re-build their country.

We entered an Egyptian restaurant on the ground floor of a shopping mall where some of our friends and colleagues from Alexandria planned to meet with us after attending the victory celebrations. On the television screen inside the restaurant we could view the news of Victory Day in Tahrir Square. From the sound system we listened to the patriotic songs that the Egyptian legend Umme Kulsum sang in the decades of the 50s and the 60s. Popular songs sung by artists like Abdul Halim Hafez and Muhammad Mounir were heard as well.

While waiting for our friends we thought of the ancient Egyptians who had impressed the whole world with architectural marvels like the great pyramids, constructed in perfect alignment with the universe. These same Egyptians, perhaps influenced by the flow of the River Nile, embarked upon many a revolution against oppression perpetrated sometimes by the pharaohs themselves, and at other times by foreign occupiers such as the Turks, French or the British. History seemed to be coming full circle today.

When our colleagues arrived, our discussion turned to the future of Egypt. All were of the opinion that the mere resignation of Mubarak and the fall of his regime would not be sufficient to change the fate of the Egyptians. What was needed now was a complete overhaul of the system of Egyptian government. If Egypt fails to construct a political structure that can sustain a truly representative and pro-people government, it will turn out to be another Philippines or an Indonesia. Twenty-five years back, in this very month of February, the corrupt dictatorial rule of Marcos had fallen in the face a turbulent revolution in the Philippines. Now, exactly twenty-five years later, there has not been much change in the structure or function of the Philippine political or economic culture. The state power has continued to change hands between a handful of influential families and a coterie of greedy power-mongers. Like the Philippines, Indonesia, also, could not bail herself out from under the curse of poverty and corruption. The fall of Suharto, their ruthless dictator, was followed by a succession of many similar despots.

One participant expressed "The situation in Egypt is different from that which we find in countries like Iran. Unlike Iran, we did not go for our revolution in order to establish a religion-based state under a spiritual leader. Men and women of all religions, opinions, classes and creeds were in the vanguard of this revolution. Together, as one Egyptian nation, we launched a peaceful revolution. And, the success attained in this peaceful revolution has to be maintained through peaceful means as well."

I responded by sharing my opinion that behind every revolutionary development in the world, good or bad, there is a set of precipitating circumstances. Every cause has its effect; every effect has its cause. Iran would not have advanced towards establishing a religion-based conservative government system through a bloody mass revolution had the democratic government under Dr. Mohammad Mosaddegh, the then Iranian Prime Minister, not been toppled by a British-American conspiracy. Dr. Mosaddegh, in 1951, nationalized the British controlled oil corporation that for decades had been expropriating oil, the major national resource of Iran. This oil corporation had also oppressed Iranian oil workers in many ways. Immediately after the nationalization took place, a conspiracy was initiated to depose Dr. Mosaddegh, the honest, courageous and patriotic Prime Minister who had been elected by almost 90 percent of the popular vote. But there was huge public support for the democratic Dr. Mosaddegh, who was truly a people's representative and whose leadership was highly acclaimed in the international arena. In August 1953 the Central Intelligence Agency of America (CIA), in collaboration with Iranian King Shah and his agents, had drafted "Operation Ajax", the elaborate plan to oust Dr. Mosaddegh. The American embassy in Tehran was turned into the headquarters of this international conspiracy and the British-American axis began manipulating public opinion. On 19 August 1953, the democratically elected government of Iranian Prime Minister Mohammad Mosaddegh was overthrown through an orchestrated coup d'état and, in defiance of the Iranian constitution, the puppet king Mohammad Reza Shah Pahlavi was seated as the ruler of Iran. Thus a conspiracy that was hatched at both national and international levels, materialized and resulted in a flood of blood of innocent people on the roads of Iran, the murdering and secret killing of thousands of Mosaddegh supporters and the home confinement of Dr. Mosaddegh, the elected Prime Minister. The irony was that Dr. Mosaddegh, who had committed his whole life to safeguarding the sovereignty of his nation, was adjudged a traitor through a staged military trial and breathed his last breath after serving fourteen years in solitary confinement. As a corollary to this unbridled example of imperialistic intervention, the world had to witness another Iranian blood-letting in 1979. This time for another revolution that yielded a theocratic government with support from the majority of its people through an electoral and parliamentary process.

While we were engrossed in a lively discussion about the history of Iran I recalled a prediction made by Dr. Mosaddegh after he was convicted. He foresaw that his fate would serve as an example in the future for freeing the Middle East from the bondage of slavery to colonial interests.[1] Indeed, the time has arrived for the chains of imperialism to be broken. Like a house of cards falling down, the forts and palaces of puppet governments run by ruthless rulers forcibly installed by the imperialist forces have already started falling apart. In this age of satellite and Internet, news is spreading at the speed of electrons and in the process the light of truth is breaking the darkness of lies, falsehoods and deceptions.

Our discussion gathered heat and momentum. Alaa was humming along with a patriotic song that was being played in the restaurant. I asked him which incident in Egypt he thought, based on his own personal experiences, was something Egyptians should feel most proud of. Alaa promptly replied: "The mass revolution in Tahrir Square. I deem the revolution an incident much more significant than that of the 6th of October war. Because, in comparison, this revolution took place through a peaceful process; every Egyptian participating in this revolution took the principle of peace as a motto embraced in their hearts."

On the 6th of October in 1973, Egypt had been victorious against the Israeli aggression. But, the people of the present generation, who grew up hearing a variety of anecdotes about the victory of 6th of October, wanted this revolution to be an inextinguishable flame that would illuminate the pathway to their future—a peaceful and democratic road to progress and prosperity.

In the evening we were invited by Susan Blankhart, the Ambassador of the Netherlands, to attend a dinner at her residence in Cairo. We had been introduced to her and her family when she was ambassador of Netherlands in Costa Rica. Amr became quite friendly with Susan and her husband, Yke Berkouwer.

After crossing the guard post, as soon as we reached the entrance, Susan and Yke received us very cordially. Yke is by profession a physician who has currently been working as a volunteer doctor at a hospital in Cairo. While Susan is warm and sprightly in her behavior, Yke is more calm and reserved.

---

[1] http://www.mohammadmossadegh.com/biography/

Ancient trees and creepers densely encircled their old mansion house. The antiquity of the trees and architectural details of the house bore ample testimony to the nobility of the families who inhabited this mansion since its construction. We sat on an open terrace that overlooked a lush green, impeccably manicured lawn. The full moon, shining like a silver plate, flooded the surrounding nature with beams of light. Situated in this charming atmosphere with a moderate evening temperature that was neither warm nor chilly, the setting offered an excellent opportunity for further conversation.

While we were immersed in our talk Susan reminded her husband to bring the appetizers from the table. Yke came with sorbets, crackers and nuts for us. As it was an off day for their domestic aides, the couple was serving us personally throughout the entire dinner. In spite of having been placed in the high official position of ambassador, Susan, along with her husband, were not at all hesitant about serving as our attendants. Such a humble attitude would be rare in any of the high profile personalities living in a society based on a rigid class hierarchy. During the meal we were served a full course dinner. In addition to the famous Netherlands potatoes the delicious feast included beef stew, casserole of vegetables, salad, and Chinese chow min.

Susan informed us about what had happened in Egypt during the last few weeks. She had not been able to enjoy good sleeps for the entire time. She was busy day and night with the task of sending Dutch citizens home with the help of the Dutch embassy.

From Susan, we came to understand a clearer picture of the brutality of the security forces during the demonstrations in Tahrir Square. Virtually trapped inside a hotel adjacent to the Tahrir Square the Dutch journalists, like other foreign reporters, had also faced threats from the security apparatuses of the Egyptian government. Along with them was Anderson Cooper, the popular host of CNN AC 360, who had boarded in the Hotel Marriot.

More than 400 innocent men, women and children were killed at the hands of the government forces. Scores of human rights workers were kidnapped and placed in unknown places. The majority of those kidnapped are yet to be traced.

Enraged at the brutality of the Egyptian security forces, Susan, in strongly worded letters, asked for a detailed report on the violation of human rights from the Egyptian foreign ministry. In each of their replies to her letters, the foreign ministry informed Susan that the ministry was not obliged to give her an answer as she did not use diplomatic language in her letters of allegation. I was curious to know from Susan what the foreign ministry actually meant accusing her of undiplomatic language. A veteran diplomat, Susan told us that, because she had directly asked for an explanation from the Egyptian government on allegations of human rights violations instead of couching the wording of her letters in diplomatic protocol, the Egyptian foreign ministry had given her such brusque replies.

It was about half an hour past ten at night when we had left the residence of the ambassador. As we started our twenty-minute walk towards Tahir Square, we took a side lane as a shortcut to reach the main road. The lane was dark but we didn't feel insecure walking through the side streets. No policemen were visible anywhere as we crossed two famous bridges, one after another. The second bridge, Qasr El-Nil, was a key passage from Zamalek and Giza to Tahrir Square. These were the bridges where military check-posts were deployed during the demonstrations. Millions of people, defying the barriers of these check-posts, had crossed the bridges and gathered in the Tahrir Square to see the fall of the autocratic government. Huge portraits of Mubarak were once hung on the roadsides. Now there was no trace of those portraits. The pictures of the dictator, which were prominently displayed in Cairo and elsewhere in Egypt, had all been removed or erased in such a way that one couldn't find the slightest trace or shadow of them.

The Nile under the moon light.

The moon overhead had climbed further up in the sky. Already fifteen days into the Arabic month of Rabiul Awaal, the full moon appeared to be signifying the fullness of the revolution. The victory of the Egyptian revolution seemed to glow with sublime purity in the beauty of the moonlight. It looked as if the moon was swimming in the River Nile, leaving in its wake millions of twinkling ripples dancing on the water's surface. At a distance, the luxury boats were idling along the river while rocking in waves of joy. Hand in hand Amr and I were slowly advancing towards Tahrir Square moving with a crowd of millions of revelers. The calm and orderly atmosphere that we saw in Tahrir Square during the day was not there in that same square at night. The youths were joyfully dancing at different corners of the square. Fireworks were set off all around.

The BBC, in one of its news broadcasts, termed the revolution a "Funny Revolution". Now, after viewing the comical behaviors of some of the victory celebrators, I think BBC did not go overboard. "Funny Revolution" was not an exaggeration. The Egyptian people are basically very jovial, with a good sense of humor; they enjoy cracking jokes. While Egyptians were in all seriousness sacrificing everything for the success of the revolution, they never missed a chance to insert a joke or spice up their conversations with a bit of humor. Looking at some of the banners and posters displayed during the demonstrations in the Tahrir Square one could get a taste of the Egyptian sense of humor. On one banner held high by a youth was written: "Go, Mubarak, go; my hands are aching from holding this banner." Another banner stated: "Go, Mubarak, go; I need to take a shower." And on yet another was inscribed: "My wife is sweating over her labor pain; but my baby is loath to get born lest the newborn has to see your face. So, go away, Mubarak, go."

Another noticeable aspect of the revolution was how, in the tumult of the demonstrations, Egyptian people still remembered and showed profound respect to their former president, Gamal Abdel Nasser. Many demonstrators carried posters with a portrait of Nasser. The then President of Egypt Nasser along with the then Prime Minister of India Nehru and the then President of Yugoslavia Tito had pioneered the international nonaligned movement with a view to making their independent states truly self-reliant by functioning outside the power influences of the Soviet Union and the United States. More than five million grieving Egyptians took to streets to express their agony after hearing the news that Nasser died on September 28, 1970. Never before in the history of Egypt had such a vast multitude of people gathered to pay their respects to an Egyptian president.

Nasser, by living an honest life himself, left an example of how one can remain incorruptible in spite of holding a position at the pinnacle of power. Still today many Egyptians treat Nasser and his family with the deepest respect.

Posing in front of a military tank in Tahrir Square.

More celebrations at night!

The Cleaning Revolution!

The whole of Tahrir Square at nighttime was beside itself with the joy of victory. There was mass jubilation as the square was thronged with men, women and children. Soldiers were seen helping people embark onto and disembark from armored military tanks to take pictures. I also posed in front of a tank for Amr to take a snapshot. It was almost midnight. The curfew would be in force in a short while. Soldiers were announcing the commencement time of curfew; but the crowd, lost in jubilation, did not seem to pay any heed to the announcements. Young men and women were immersed in their ordinary conversation. Some were enjoying rides on horse carts; some were busy buying popcorns, walnuts and corn-on-the-cob freshly baked in live fires. We finally left Tahrir Square at midnight.

February 19, 2011

In the morning of the next day, we set out for Alexandria, a city the Egyptians call Alex for short. Amr, Shahinaz El-Hennawi, Amira Abu-Hussain and I were in the car and in the driver's seat were Mandy Taha, an engineer by profession, who was like her compatriots in the car, dressed in hijab. Mandy was one of the organizers of the mass revolution in Alex. This women's group came from Alexandria to participate in the victory day in Tahrir Square.

One thing that attracted my attention was that almost half of the car drivers in Egypt were women and in the public places one could see many women with their hair covered by scarves of different colors. Hijab means a modest dressing for a Muslim woman covering everything except her face and hands. In public the Egyptian women are found to be comfortable with long skirts, shirts and pants having their heads covered by scarves. Women covered in a head-to-foot burqa were sometimes seen in Egypt.

My first trip to Egypt was in 1998, shortly after my marriage with Amr. Since then, I have noticed that the number of hijab-wearing women in Egypt was on the rise and nowadays a great number of Egyptian women are seen wearing hijab as their favored clothing. Interestingly, I came across families where the daughter was wearing hijab, but not the mother or one sister was clothed in hijab and the other sister wore western attire. It is their individual choice and no one frowns upon the other for wearing a different dress. According to the law in Iran and Saudi Arabia it is compulsory for women to wear hijab. But now many women in these two countries are adamantly against hijab. Some Iranian representatives I met at the international women's conference in Tehran in 1995, told me about this trend. I have also seen with my own eyes how some Saudi women cast off their hijab immediately after the airplane they were boarding had crossed their country's borders. In juxtaposition, when the Turkish government took an extreme measure against hijab, mass demonstrations ensued and it was hijab-supporting women who emerged victorious. In this regard, Egypt has chosen to take a middle course like Bangladesh, Malaysia, Indonesia and most Muslim countries where personal matters like what one should wear in public have been left entirely up to the individual to choose.

One of the fundamental truths established by Islam is that no one can be compelled to accept Islam and it is clearly mentioned in the holy Quran that" Let there be no compulsion in religion."(chapter 2: verse 256) Those who, defying this principle of Islam, have tried to control the private life of individuals mostly failed to achieve their goals. The topic of compulsion and free will has long been debated in intellectual discourses. But history has proven, time and again, that any extreme position or legally bound compulsion with respect to personal morality will not bring fruitful results.

It took four hours for us to reach Alexandria. When we entered the city a scene of groups of young men and women who were busy sweeping and painting the footpaths greeted us. Civilians engaged themselves in controlling the traffic. Seated next to me, Amira who works in the Library of Alexandria informed us that there was no police force in the whole city of Alexandria. All the police personnel had fled out of fear because, during the demonstrations, they had unleashed attacks on the innocent civilians. They were afraid of retaliation. Civilians were now in charge of enforcing law and order. Fortunately, there was no report as yet of any mishaps such as robberies or violent activities.

Along the way, Shahinaz and I were dropped off at her apartment. In her apartment I washed and changed and took a little rest. Amr went out to attend a meeting. Shahinaz, the young professor of the Institute of Peace Studies, decorated her apartment nicely with tasteful interiors and furniture, all mildly painted and varnished. She separated one room exclusively for her prayers and meditations. A statuette in a posture of Sufi dancing decorated her bedroom. The Sufi poet Mowlana Jalaluddin Rumi introduced Sufi dancing or a ritual of moving around in a circle with beating drums, as a spiritual practice for meditation. Decorative frames holding paintings and inspirational quotations also adorned the walls of her rooms for meditation.

At six in the evening about fifteen of us gathered together at the popular Hosni Restaurant, a favorite eatery of both Amr and myself. The city of Alexandria, located on the Mediterranean coast, is especially famous for delicious fish. Fish fried with garlic, cumin seeds and parsley leaves were served along with pita breads and Fattoush Salad made of cucumber, lettuce, tomato, parsley leaves, and an ambrosia of curd and garlic sauce. Besides this, there was Tameya (which is also known as Falafel) a kind of deep fried ball or patty made from fava or garbanzo beans; and Fattah, a dish made of flatbread as a foundation upon which yogurt, garlic, rice and other ingredients are added. Some of us also placed orders for meat dishes like Kebab and stuffed vegetable dishes like Kusa Mahshya (stuffed zucchini dolma).

A young professor from the Alexandria's Institute of Peace Studies, Mr. Bassem Maher, and his wife Sara Nader, also came to the party; Sara was holding her newborn daughter in her lap. Bassem and Sara are both Christians. They chose the name Malika for their daughter as the name bears a particular significance in Arabic. The word is taken from the classical Arabic word Malak meaning Angel, which has also been used, in the holy Quran.

Our friends Bassem, Sarah and their daughter Malika.

There are many Christians in Egypt and there is a noticeable inter-personal fraternity between Muslims and Christians. In the Arab world the word Allah means God to every religion. Both Christians and Muslims call their God by the common Arabic name Allah. The first city that the first missionary from Palestine, the birthplace of Jesus (peace be upon him), visited was this ancient city of Alex. Like Bassem and Sara, most Egyptian Christians are Coptic Christians who are the descendants of the earliest Christians. The Coptic Christians observe the 7th of January as the birthday of Jesus (peace be upon him).

I asked Bassem what he thought about the church bombing on the New Year's Eve. Bassem said, quoting the British ambassador, the BBC reported that the former Home Minister, Habib Al Adli, who is now under house arrest and facing trial, was involved in the church bombing. Bassem himself does not believe that the so-called "Muslim" terrorists were behind the bombing. Those who were in the party also seconded Bassem's opinion because, if the so-called "Muslim" terrorists were involved then more churches would have been attacked during the 18-day demonstrations when there was practically no effective police force to guard the city. In fact, Mubarak's government policy was to use the "Muslim" terrorist threat while clinging to power with international support.

Karim Mahrous and his wife Iman Gaballah (in Arabic culture and also in Islamic practice a wife does not have to use her husband's name as her surname) came with their baby son Mustafa. Karim, who also participated in the mass revolution in Alex, was badly beaten when he attempted to rescue a woman from police attack.

With friends at Hosni Restaurant in Alexandria, Egypt.

Mohammad Abu-Shaqra, a lawyer by training and an advocate of peace and justice, said he was initially hesitant about participating in the mass revolution of January 25th. But, he steeled himself after what he heard from a cab driver. During their conversation the cab driver said to him: "This revolution is our last chance to rid our society of corruption and injustice." The cab driver further said that although he might lose one day's wage if he joined the demonstrations, still for the sake of his family's future and for the welfare of his nation he must join in to make a success of the revolution.

Many of Amr's students were contemplating the establishment of a non-governmental organization that would identify social problems and find peaceful solutions for immediate implementation.[2] They also discussed the issue of how to encourage, in near future, a cordial relationship between police forces and citizens that would foster mutual respect and confidence. In this regard they were planning to begin work by holding training workshops. They were focused on ways to establish peaceful communications between all groups.

---

2   Since then they officially established the organization: Mediation for Community Development.

With no police force to guard the city, there had already been several reports of lawlessness in some areas of Alexandria. A few people were unlawfully extending the boundaries of their homes. Some were even taking illegal possession of open spaces. Although citizens had been deeply concerned about the potential for chaos and confusion, still, the situation had not yet gotten out of control.

The students, eager to form civil organizations, were soliciting guidance from Amr. After consultations with his students Amr decided he would come back in the coming March when he could be with them to help form well-structured activities for the newly established non-governmental organization.

We boarded the 10:30 night train from Alexandria and reached Cairo only three hours later. At 1:30 in the dead of night Cairo was still wide awake and pulsating with the movement of its people. No one could say that there was a successful curfew in force at that time!

February 20, 2011

The next day was Sunday, the 20th of February. Many people came to the hotel lobby to meet us. Justice Mahmoud Mourad came with his wife Yomna Abd-El Hamid. Yomna teaches English at American University in Cairo which was now temporarily closed due to the upheaval. She believes that an Islamic constitution based on the Islamic principles of fairness and justice can ensure the rights of Egyptian citizens of different faiths. Justice Mahmoud was deeply concerned that the success of this revolution might not be sustained for long if civil organizations drawn from all sections of the people could not be formed immediately. The Egyptian judiciary is still held in high esteem. Many institutions in Egypt had fallen victim to the greedy influence of the Mubarak government, but the judiciary in many respects could still maintain a measure of independence in their functioning. The education and judicial sectors of many countries have been politicized and made to serve the partisan interests and petty whims of the party in power.

Many of Amr's friends and former colleagues are now placed in high positions of the judiciary. Highly admired by the Egyptians, Judge Ali Al-Hawary, a friend of Amr, is now the chief prosecutor of public funds. His job is to collect all the evidences and legal documents before framing a case on misappropriation of public funds by the Mubarak government. Another friend of Amr is the Attorney-General of Egypt, Abdel Magid Mahmoud. The Egyptian people earnestly hope that Abdel Magid will take stern measures against the alleged corruptions of the Mubarak government and will do his best to uphold justice and ensure fair play.

Justice Mahmoud and Amr discussed various methods to organize and strengthen civil society in Egypt. They also discussed the possibility of infusing the philosophical concept of conflict resolution and peace studies into the day-to-day activities of the judicial department. The young judge Mahmoud seemed quite enthusiastic about the idea.

Based on what I learned from our discussions with people during the last few days, I think the majority of Egyptians deemed the former foreign minister Amr Musa the fittest candidate to be the new Egyptian President.[3] Not withstanding the fact that he had served in the Mubarak government as a minister, Amr Musa's efficiency and honesty had earned respect and admiration among the Egyptian people. Many believe that Mubarak, either fearing or envying Amr Musa's popularity in Egypt, had hastily removed him from his ministerial job and placed him outside the country as the head of Arab League. Amr Musa is no longer holding that position in Arab League.

Egyptian youth believe that the revolution has not ended; rather, it has just started. The Egyptian political system needs to be totally dismantled and reestablished with a truly pro-people government. Until then, the revolution should continue unabated. I had noticed that among many Egyptians there were mixed feelings about the Muslim Brotherhood (Ikhwanul Muslemin), the influential political party that still has support at the grassroots of Egyptian society. Founded in Egypt in 1928 by Hassan al-Banna, a schoolteacher, the Muslim Brotherhood gained great respect throughout the Arab world in the middle of the last century for its political idealism combined with Islamic charity works. But the Muslim Brotherhood became highly controversial later after the party chose a course of violence. In 1948, the party was banned by the then Prime Minister of Egypt for its violent activities. In retaliation for the banning of the party, one Brotherhood activist assassinated the prime minister. In the same year the founder of Brotherhood, Hassan al-Banna, was also assassinated. It is assumed that supporters of the assassinated Prime Minister or any of his pro-government forces most likely killed Banna as yet another act of reprisal.

In a bloodless coup d'état in 1952 Gamal Abdel Nasser came to power through "The Free Officers' Movement" by removing King Farouk who was subservient to British imperialism. Ideological conflict between Nasser and the Brotherhood was mounting. In 1954, Nasser while addressing a public meeting in Alexandria was the target of an assassination plot. He narrowly escaped death from a gunshot by an unknown assassin. The government, however, blamed the Brotherhood for the assassination attempt.

---

3   Such views have changed a lot since then.

Egyptians regained their lost pride in 1956 when Nasser nationalized the British-occupied Suez Canal. For his resolute stand against the colonial and imperialist forces Nasser emerged as a Third-World hero. To the Brotherhood, however, Nasser was a brute and an autocrat, in spite of the pride and fame he had earned in national and international arenas. The security apparatuses of Nasser had tortured and confined thousands of Brotherhood members on the grounds that the Brotherhood's political philosophy was retrogressive, that they attempted to kill Nasser and that they were conspiring with American imperialist forces to topple the Egyptian government.

Brotherhood leader Sayyid Qutb was accused of plotting to overthrow the Nasser government through violence and was sentenced to death in a trial which was termed a farce by many Brotherhood loyalists in the Arab world. On 29 August 1966, Sayyid Qutb was executed by hanging. During that transitional period members of the Brotherhood became friendly with members of the Saudi Royal family as well as with the supporters of Saudi Wahabism, known for its narrow interpretations of Islam. Thousands of oppressed Brotherhood members in Egypt took shelter in Saudi Arabia and in the United States. In Bangladesh the religiously-based political party Jamaat-e-Islami, who colluded with Pakistan military forces responsible for 1971 genocide, mass-rape and plunder in Bangladesh, was also influenced by the extreme political philosophy of Sayyid Qutb and the ultra-conservative Wahabi school of thought.

In 1970, the Brotherhood declared that they had eschewed the path of violence. Traveling a long political road, passing through many divergences and re-emergences, the Muslim Brotherhood has of late settled back into their main goal: education and human welfare in the light of Islam. The Muslim Brotherhood won many seats in the 2005 parliamentary election. But the Mubarak government once again declared the political party outlawed. Mohammed Badie, the present leader of Brotherhood, announced that they would not be contesting in the up-coming election for the Egyptian presidency. He said: "Our aim is only to help everybody in establishing democracy, social justice and peace." Many observers have been reassured by this announcement; but many are still not sure about the ultimate goal of the Muslim Brotherhood.[4]

The topic of Arab unity was also broached. If European countries that have been torn by war after war for centuries can be united to form a European Union, introducing a common currency and allowing their people speaking in different languages to cross their borders as they wish without any visa, why can't the Arab world, with its people all speaking in the same language, be united? Arab countries that have recently gotten rid of their autocratic governments could at least take the

---

[4] However, the Muslim Brotherhood ended up nominating a candidate for the 2012 presidential election.

lead to unite the Arab world by first uniting themselves. The biggest obstacle to Arab unity, needless to say, will come from the western corporate powers that have planted puppet governments all over the Middle East in order to loot and grab resources and properties. Interestingly, as I returned to Washington I was amazed to learn in the news media that people in the Arab world have already started discussing the idea of an Arab Union with a common Arab currency.

After spending the day in the hotel, holding meetings, engaging in casual conversations, and small talk with friends and relatives, we along with Alaa and his two sons, Mohammad and Mustafa, went to Rehab City, about 40 minutes from Cairo. In Rehab we visited Amr's childhood friend and neighbor Hossam Fahmy and his wife Dalia Khalil. Hossam is a physician by profession. He is a professor of Ain Shams College of Medicine in Cairo. Dalia is completing a PhD degree in Education from the United States and, vis-à-vis has founded a youth organization in Cairo focusing on peace and development. Dalia explained that the leadership of this mass revolution was not in the control of any one individual's hand. People, in response to different situations, spontaneously shouldered leadership as and when it was necessary in a variety of ways through the force of circumstances. Mainly educated people took over leadership from the middle-class and the lower middle-class sections of the society. Those who belong to the disadvantaged groups and are extremely poor, who make their ends meet by menial jobs, did not come into the picture as leaders though they, like the general masses, had also started weaving new dreams revolving around the revolution. If, for any reason, this revolution fails to give expected positive results and if people ultimately find their dreams are not coming true, it is feared that the peaceful revolution may then give way to an ominous class revolution, spilling blood.

Hossam said that when he went to join the demonstrations in Tahrir Square, he and other fellow civilians had an uphill struggle while crossing the high security guard posts; but those who came riding camels and horses from the pyramid areas in Gaza, 15/16 kilometers away, did not face any obstacle to getting clearance from the security officers to invade the crowds in Tahrir Square. I mentioned to Hossam about the camel drivers who the other day distributed leaflets asking for pardon and convened a meeting in Tahrir Square where they were to ask for forgiveness.

On our return to Heliopolis we went to the residence of another of Amr's boyhood friends, Mohsin Khattab and his wife Nabila El-Wediny, to attend their 30th marriage anniversary celebration. Other invitees included their common friend Magdi Sultan, who came accompanied by his two daughters, Nivene and Nadine. Sitting around the dining table conversations began and, once again, the topic of discussion revolved around Tahrir Square. The story of the revolution in Egypt, the greatest revolution of the 21st century, seemed unending.

A Revolution of the Heart

It was already 2 at night when we returned to our hotel room. The next day we were to fly for the United States by Egypt Air. I asked Amr: "Can you tell me what the greatest wonder of this revolution was?" Amr, with his usual half-smile, kept quiet and gave me a questioning glance; I said: "The greatest wonder of this revolution, at least to my eyes, was the self-immolation of Mohammed Bouazizi, the Tunisian fruit seller. His act of sacrificing his life in protest of injustice, harassment and humiliation had sparked the mass revolutions in the whole Arab world. This revolution will perhaps be noted in the history as the catalyst for the future victories of the lovers of peace and justice all over the world!

The End

Edwards Brothers Malloy
Thorofare, NJ USA
October 3, 2012